30 DAILY DEVOTIONS

WHAT'S IN YOUR ROOM?

Cover photo: Kerri Herner
Art direction and design: Rule29
Editor: Dale Reeves
Project Editor: Lindsay Black

Library of Congress Cataloging-in-Publication Data:

Kast, Michael, 1966-
     What's in your room? : 30 daily devotions / Michael Kast.-- 1st ed.
        p. cm.
    "Empowered Youth Products."
       Includes index.
     ISBN 0-7847-1736-2 (pbk.)
1. High school students--Prayer-books and devotions--English. 2. Christian teenagers--Prayer-books and devotions--English. 3. Devotional calendars. I. Title.

BV4850.K376 2005
242'.63--dc22

           2005007222

Standard Publishing, Cincinnati, Ohio.
A division of Standex International Corporation.
All rights reserved.

12   11   10   09   08   07   06   05   7   6   5   4   3   2   1

ISBN 0-7847-1736-2

30 DAILY DEVOTIONS

WHAT'S IN YOUR ROOM?

Michael Kast

EMPOWERED® Youth Products
Standard Publishing | Cincinnati, Ohio

DEDICATION

I'd like to dedicate this book to my mom. You were always there to "encourage" me to keep my room clean. Thanks for everything, even the weekly "white glove inspections" that drove me crazy. The lessons you taught me about taking care of my room are helping me keep my life and family in order today. I love you. Proverbs 22:6

Your son,

Michael

—not to protect those who have made foolish mistakes, but to protect those of us who claim to have known them.

CONTENTS

INTRODUCTION

I t seems that my life gets busier and busier all the time. It gets harder and harder to find time just to relax. I love to sit on the deck and take some time to unwind. It gives me a chance to reflect on my day, think about my family and remember what is most important to me.

As I think back through my life, I have always had a "special place." But the place that I felt the most at home when I was growing up was my bedroom. I spent a ton of time in there, doing my homework, relaxing, playing computer games, listening to music, sleeping—everything. My room was where I felt comfortable and safe. My room was where I relaxed, planned, worried, worked, dreamed and played. It was a great place.

Almost everything in my room had some kind of meaning to me. Whether it was the soccer trophy on the shelf, the pictures of my friends on the wall, the desk where I did my homework or the science project growing out of the leftover pizza under my bed—I loved my room. My room said a lot about who I was. It reflected my interests, my personality and my character. If you spent a little time in my bedroom, you would learn a lot about me.

For the next thirty days this book will take a look at different items that—more likely than not—are in your room. Each item can help you learn a little bit about yourself and God. So sit back, grab your Bible and take a journey to know God better—without even leaving your room!

HOW TO USE THIS BOOK

This book is not designed to be read in one sitting. In fact, it is intended for you to read one chapter a day and be able to think about just one aspect of your life each day for thirty days.

Getting started

Just by having this book, you have taken a huge step. Whether you bought it on your own, or it was given to you as a gift, you are on the edge of a great adventure with God. Don't put it off any longer—dive right in.

Pick a time

View this time as an appointment with God. If you forget, you are breaking your promise to God that you'd meet with him. Don't forget—he's always there for you and will never break his appointment with you.

Pick a place

Think about a place where you can spend ten to fifteen uninterrupted minutes concentrating on your relationship with God. Maybe that's in your room, or maybe it's at the breakfast table. Wherever it is, claim it as your special place where you will come to meet God each day.

Get ready

As you go through this book, you will need a Bible and something to write with. Before you start, spend some time asking God to help you keep your appointment. Ask him to make this time valuable for you so that you can walk away each day with one area to think about throughout the day.

Each day

You will need to set aside about ten to fifteen minutes for each day. You'll read a short story that introduces the thought for the day. Then you'll read from your Bible in the ENTERING IN section that will bring the lesson to life. The GETTING IT RIGHT section will bring out the lessons for you to focus on each day. In the LIVING IT OUT section you will have the time to answer questions that will help you identify one or two things that you can do during that day. You'll wrap up each appointment with the TALKING TO GOD section—this is your chance to talk directly to God and hear from him. So make sure that you finish strong and are ready to listen to God's direction.

I want to encourage you to be open and honest with yourself and God as you work your way through this book. No one will see this but you, unless you choose to show it to someone. The next time you take a minute to really look at your bedroom, remember that your room is full of lessons from God to help get you through the day.

DAY 1 | AQUARIUM
Freedom in Christ

I used to have a fish aquarium in my room. The ten-gallon tank sat on a stand next to my desk, and it was my job to feed the fish and keep the tank clean. I loved to sit and watch my Black Moors, Red Orandas and Bubble Eyes swimming through the plastic plants and fake rocks.

One day as I watched the fish, I realized that I had brought them home from the pet store in a small plastic bag and carefully put them in my ten-gallon tank. They were perfectly content to live out the rest of their existence there. The fish had no concept of larger bodies of water—twenty-gallon tanks, bathtubs, ponds, lakes or oceans.

If you've ever seen the movie *Finding Nemo*, you know that at one point Nemo is captured and put into a dentist's aquarium. He is to be a birthday gift for the dentist's niece Darlene. Knowing that Darlene has a history of shaking her fish to death, Nemo and all of his friends make several attempts to escape. While many of his tank friends had never experienced an outside body of water, Nemo had. He knew that he didn't belong in a tank, but in an ocean. I'd like to tell you that Nemo and his friends escape to the ocean, but I don't want to ruin the movie for you—in case you haven't seen it yet.

But sometimes we are a lot like ten-gallon fish—we settle for staying in our little tanks and we don't even try to take advantage of opportunities to make it to the ocean. That reminds me of a story I heard years ago. At a farmer's market in a little village there was a small group of quail, called a covey, walking in circles around a pole. They had strings attached to their legs to ensure that they would not fly away. They continued to walk around and around the pole hour after hour. A man came into the market and asked, "How much will you take for all of them?" Once they agreed on a price, he paid the owner. Then he began to cut the strings off of their legs. "What are you doing?" the owner asked in disbelief. "I'm setting them free," said the new owner.

The strange thing was that even though the man had cut the strings and given them their freedom, the quail continued to walk around the pole just as they had done before. They failed to realize that they were free to break out of the circle and fly away.

Sometimes we act like quail that don't understand that the strings that bound us have been cut. We get so used to our own world, family and school that we start to put limits on God. We get comfortable with the ordinary events of life. We stop thinking about the fact that God exists outside our world. God created the world. God created me. God created you. God can do anything. But God didn't create us to be like ten-gallon fish. God has a great plan for your life. So stop limiting God with ten-gallon ideas and dive into the vast ocean of his power.

ENTERING IN

The Israelites had been taken from their homes and were living in exile in a foreign land. Most likely, they were upset and somewhat down. So the prophet Jeremiah wrote to remind them that no matter how bad things got, God still had a plan for them. Read Jeremiah 29:11-13.

GETTING IT RIGHT

What do you think God is trying to tell you about the difference between his plan and our expectations for our daily lives? When you read this promise, what do you think of?

_____

_____

_____

_____

_____

_____

_____

_____

_____

_____

_____

LIVING IT OUT

How can you apply this lesson of God's plan for you to your life now?

_____

_____

_____

_____

_____

_____

TALKING TO GOD

Take some time to thank God for having a good plan for your life. Thank him for not forgetting you when life gets a little tough. Thank him for having a greater plan when our ten-gallon plan seems to fall apart.

_____

_____

_____

_____

_____

_____

_____

_____

_____

_____

_____

_____

_____

_____

OTHER THOUGHTS

_____

_____

_____

DAY 2 | LAMP
Light in a dark world

T alk about pressure! Have you ever had a class in which your final exam made up a large percent of your final grade? When I took wood shop, we had to complete a project that could be used in our homes. It was graded and accounted for ninety percent of the final grade—ouch! I chose to make a lamp that I could keep close to my bed so that I would finally stop running into things when I got up during the night. So I got to work and began the process of constructing the lamp.

I glued up some wood strips and mounted them on the lathe. Using the lathe, I rounded the block into a straight column. Then I began to work the wood by cutting and shaping valleys in the spindle. After I achieved the shape I needed for the lamp column, I slowed the lathe and began the sanding process. I started off with coarse 60-grit sandpaper and worked up to very fine 220-grit. When the sanding was finished, I mounted the column on the drill press and drilled a hole exactly through the middle of the entire piece. Then I installed the wire and the electrical socket to complete the project.

I ended up getting an A- on the project. But I was so proud of my lamp that you would have thought that I had gotten a perfect score. I still remember the day that I brought home my lamp. I cleared off a place on the nightstand next to my bed, plugged it in and stood back to admire my creation. It looked great!

I used the lamp all the time. Each night the light from that lamp would fill my room as I got ready for bed. Once I was in bed, I would reach over and turn it off, turning my room completely dark. The first thing I would do each morning was reach over and turn on the light so that I could save my feet from brutal encounters with my bedroom furniture.

But after a few months, something happened to my lamp. For some reason it wouldn't work all of the time. When I turned the knob, sometimes it would work, and other times it wouldn't. It even got to the point that it would suddenly turn itself off. It was more than a little annoying that I couldn't depend on my lamp to do what I had created it to do. I put my lamp on a shelf in the closet and never used it again.

A few months later, my mom bought another lamp for me, and I replaced my handmade lamp with a more reliable one. I guess a lamp that doesn't work isn't worth very much.

Sometimes we are like lamps that don't always work when we're supposed to. We make mistakes and let people down. But more than that, we let God down. Jesus said that we are created to be lights for God in the world today. And he also talked about how ineffective a light is that no one can see. We need to let God be our source of light so that the world won't have to live in darkness.

ENTERING IN

Read Matthew 5:14-16. Jesus says that Christians are a light in a dark world. He goes on to say that people should see the good things that we do and praise God.

_____

_____

_____

_____

GETTING IT RIGHT

How does it make you feel to know that you are a light to the world?

_____

_____

_____

_____

_____

_____

_____

What type of light would you say your life is? Is it a candle—pretty, but easily blown out? Is it a strobe light—exciting, but sporadic? Is it a flashlight—works great when the batteries have power? Is it a spot-light—strong and consistent and plugged into a reliable source of power?

_____

_____

_____

_____

_____

_____

_____

_____

_____

_____

_____

_____

What kind of light do you want to be?

_____

_____

_____

_____

_____

_____

_____

_____

LIVING IT OUT

Now reread verses 14-16 and notice that our light is to shine and
people are to see it. But our actions are to point people toward God
and not ourselves. Would you say that your actions draw more
attention to God or more attention to yourself?

_____

_____

_____

_____

_____

_____

_____

_____

_____

Why did you give the answer you did?

_____

_____

_____

_____

_____

_____

_____

_____

_____

What is one way that you can have your light shine more for God and less toward you?

_____

_____

_____

_____

_____

_____

_____

_____

_____

_____

_____

TALKING TO GOD

Pray that God would help you have a strong and consistent light for him. Also ask that he will help the focus of your good actions be for him and not yourself.

_____

_____

_____

_____

_____

_____

_____

_____

_____

OTHER THOUGHTS

_____

_____

_____

_____

_____

_____

_____

_____

DAY 3 | PHONE
The words we use

One year for Christmas my parents gave my sister her own phone as a gift. She had been begging for a phone for months, and they kept telling her that she was too young to have her own phone. Finally Christmas day came and she opened her present, and there it was—her very own phone. She couldn't believe it. She ripped open the box and ran to her room to plug it in and start talking to her friends. And that was the beginning of what seemed like one never-ending phone call.

I often asked my sister who she was talking to and what they were saying during their hours of hushed conversations. She said that she was talking to her friends and that what they were talking about was none of my business. So I did what any big brother would do, I started sneaking up to the door of her room and eavesdropping on her conversations. I found that most of her discussions centered on her friends, other girls and cute guys—I didn't listen too long after they started talking about that last one.

One day I passed by my sister's room while she was talking to her friend Rachel. I heard them mention "Zeus," which was the nickname of one of my friends, so I stopped and listened. I could only catch some of what was being said, but the conversation was basically about how he was getting on Rachel's nerves. She apparently said that he was always running around on her, that he was constantly begging her for things and that he was too old for her.

I couldn't stand there and listen to them talk that way about my friend Rodney Zeustiac any longer. So I burst into the room and confronted my sister. My sister sat there, holding the phone in silence for a moment and then she burst into laughter. When she finally regained control, she explained to me that they were not talking about my friend, but about Rachel's dog Zeus. I was totally embarrassed. Even though I had tried to save my friend's reputation by interrupting the conversation, I had been eavesdropping and had jumped in without knowing all of the facts.

When I think of all the conversations that I have, either on the phone or in person, I begin to realize that not all of the words I use are positive, helpful and good. In fact, I talk about other people too much and can be downright nasty!

There are many ways that I can use my words to hurt others. Sometimes I don't tell the whole truth, or I shade the truth to put myself in a better light than those I'm talking to. Other times, I get angry with people and say words that are really bad! And I've gotten pretty good at using sarcasm in my humor to rip someone to shreds. I don't know if you are like me at all, but I have a hard time controlling my words. I sure could use some help to speak more positively!

ENTERING IN
Read Ephesians 4:25-29. As you read, make a list of all the different aspects of our speech that are covered in today's text.

_____

_____

_____

_____

_____

GETTING IT RIGHT

Today's text covers many facets of our verbal communications. Lying, truth telling, angry words, unwholesome talk and encouragement are just a few. If God attached a tape recorder to your telephone and played it for your parents or youth minister, would you be embarrassed about anything you said? What?

_____

_____

_____

_____

_____

_____

_____

_____

Why would you be embarrassed?

_____

_____

_____

_____

_____

_____

LIVING IT OUT

Make a list of everything positive that you say to others this day.
Make another list of all the derogatory, disparaging or offensive things
you say.

Which list is longer? How do you feel about each list?

When is it hardest for you to say positive things?

_____

_____

_____

_____

_____

_____

_____

_____

What can you do to make your negative list nonexistent?

_____

_____

_____

_____

_____

_____

_____

_____

_____

TALKING TO GOD

Today we have been talking about our words. Don't start off your prayer using the exact same words that you do every time you pray. Try to approach God in a different way each time you talk to him. Ask him to help you fulfill his instruction to speak "only what is helpful for building others up. . . . "

OTHER THOUGHTS

DAY 4 | STEREO
We need filters

'll never forget the day that I bought my first stereo. I brought it home from the store and proudly put it on my bookshelf. I plugged it in, put in my favorite CD and lay on my bed to try it out. The stereo came with its own remote control, so I pushed the "play" button, cranked up the volume and listened to the music. I was in Heaven!

I don't know how long I lay there listening to music. I also lost track of how loud the stereo was, because I was startled when my mother tapped me on the shoulder. I immediately punched off the music and quickly apologized for playing it so loudly by muttering something like, "I was just testing it out."

She sat down on my bed and asked me what I was listening to. I shrugged and said, "Just some music." She asked if she could listen with me. I was a little confused, because my mom loved Elvis Presley, and I was listening to AC/DC. I tried to act nonchalant and told her that she wouldn't like the music, but she insisted that we listen to it.

So I hit the "back" button, and the first chords of "You Shook Me All Night Long" cranked out. I turned the volume down as we sat there and listened. I had never realized how awful it feels when someone who cares about you watches you doing something that you really shouldn't be doing. I felt awful while my mom was sitting next to me listening to AC/DC. When the song ended, she said that she had trouble catching some of the words. She asked if I would write them out for her. I was horrified.

I pulled out a notebook and began writing out the words. It was pretty painful because it's a song that describes things you wouldn't want your mom to hear.

After I'd written out the entire song, my mom said, "Michael, you are a Christian. Do you think that God would be pleased by your listening to those lyrics?" Needless to say, I got my mom's point. She was telling me that I had a choice about what kinds of things I put into my mind. She was challenging me to fill my mind with good things—not bad things.

Even though that happened several years ago, every time I hear that song on the radio, I feel guilty and switch the station. That's one lesson that will hopefully stay with me for a long time.

ENTERING IN

God is all about our filling our minds with positive things and filtering out the bad stuff. Read Philippians 4:8.

GETTING IT RIGHT

This verse is telling us that we need to put a filter on everything that goes into our minds—everything we hear and see. List the qualities that are included in this filter found in today's verse.

_____

_____

_____

_____

_____

_____

_____

_____

LIVING IT OUT

As you go through the day, keep track of everything that gets caught in the Philippians 4:8 filter. Write them here tonight before you go to bed. By being aware of what you are exposed to, you are taking the first step toward thinking like God wants you to think.

_____

_____

_____

_____

_____

_____

TALKING TO GOD

As you studied today's Scripture, there were probably things that came to your mind that wouldn't get through the Philippians 4:8 filter. Take some time to ask God to give you the strength to avoid or overcome these things. Ask him to help you install a Philippians 4:8 filter.

OTHER THOUGHTS

DAY 5 | BULLETIN BOARD
Healthy priorities

I always kept a bulletin board over the desk in my bedroom so that I could keep track of things that were important to me. There were pictures of my friends from when we went camping, ticket stubs from St. Louis Cardinal baseball games, a list of phone numbers and e-mail addresses of my friends. Any ribbons that I won from soccer also went up onto the board. There was a thank-you note I received from my youth leader for helping clean up after an all-nighter. And of course I had a picture of my girlfriend right in the middle, so that I could look up at her each night as I did my homework.

All of the things I kept on my bulletin board were symbolic of the things that were most important to me. If a stranger were to come into my room, he would be able to learn quite a bit about me.

Imagine that you are going to have the opportunity to meet someone who is traveling from a foreign country. She doesn't speak English, and you don't speak a word of her language—communicating will be tough. But you can bring ten items that describe you. These ten items represent what you like, what you are good at and your priorities.

Take a minute and make a list of the ten things you would bring and what each says about you.

1. _____

_____

2. _____

_____

3. _____

_____

4. _____

_____

5. _____

_____

6. _____

_____

7. _____

_____

8. _____

_____

9. _____

_____

10. _____

_____

Now look back over your list. Are you surprised by the items that you chose? Do they accurately represent who you are? Who you want to be? Are the things that are important to you the same types of things that are important to Jesus?

ENTERING IN

When a teacher of the law tried to trick Jesus by asking him what the most important command to follow was, Jesus gave a great answer. Read about the encounter in Matthew 22:34-40.

_____

_____

GETTING IT RIGHT

Jesus said that all of the commands could be summed up in two short ones. The first was to love God. The second was to love your neighbor. If you had to give yourself a grade for how well you follow both of these commands, what would it be?

Love God _____   Love People _____

Why did you give yourself these grades?

_____

_____

_____

_____

_____

_____

_____

_____

What things do you do that would bring your grades down?

_____

_____

_____

_____

_____

_____

_____

LIVING IT OUT

Is it easier to love God or to love those around you?

_____

_____

_____

_____

_____

_____

_____

_____

_____

Why do you think that is?

_____

_____

_____

_____

_____

_____

_____

_____

_____

How can you improve on following both of these commands? Jot down a couple specific ways you can love God better.

_____

_____

_____

_____

_____

_____

_____

_____

Think of some of your "neighbors." What specific actions can you take to love them better?

_____

_____

_____

_____

_____

_____

_____

_____

_____

TALKING TO GOD

One of the ways that we can show our love for God is to talk to him. Spend a few moments sharing with him why you chose the ten items that you did. Thank him for putting these people, things and experiences in your life. Ask him to help you love him more deeply and to love people more genuinely.

_____

_____

_____

_____

_____

_____

_____

_____

OTHER THOUGHTS

_____

_____

_____

_____

_____

_____

_____

_____

_____

_____

DAY 6 | TRASH CAN
Avoiding sin

One of my chores has always been taking out the trash. The garbage truck came early on Monday mornings, so I took the trash out to the curb before I went to bed on Sunday nights. Each week the trash from my room reminded me of what I had done the week before. It might be a mistake-filled homework paper, candy bar wrappers, an old holey sock or movie ticket stubs.

But after a few years of trash duty, I was tired of collecting the household trash. So even though I still had to pick up everyone else's trash—my parents wouldn't have it any other way—I decided that I didn't need to take out the trash from my room. I let it pile up in the can, and eventually it spilled over onto the floor. My thinking was that I would take it out whenever I wanted to—as little as possible—but my trash collecting philosophy didn't last long.

I'll never forget the day that my view of my dreaded task totally changed. I was lying across my bed listening to my favorite CD. As I lay there, I noticed something on my windowsill. Upon closer inspection, I discovered that it was a trail of little ants. Being the curious type, I followed the trail. It went down the wall, under the corner of my dresser, across the carpet and under my bed. I got down on the floor and lifted my blanket to get a closer look. What I found was incredible!

I had eaten an ice cream sandwich and thrown the wrapper under my bed a few days before. By the time I found it, it had green mold growing on it and about a million little ants swarming over it. I was grossed out!

I immediately cleaned up the mess, took out the trash and doused my room with bug spray to get rid of the ants. I couldn't believe what a little trash, left for a few days, attracted.

Sometimes we let trash—sin—build up in our lives. I realized that my sin of laziness had some negative effects—thousands of ants! When we don't take our trash to the curb regularly, there's a real danger of becoming trapped in sin, and that makes it a lot harder to clean it up. To be honest, it took quite a while to get all of the ants out of my room. It seemed that once they got in, they liked it and I had to work really hard to get rid of them. It's kind of like that in our lives. When we realize that we are doing something wrong, we make changes, but the effects of our sin often remain for quite a while. It's so much better to avoid the sin in the first place than to have to clean up afterward.

ENTERING IN

Just like I needed to take out the trash to keep out the ants, we have things that clutter up our lives. Read Hebrews 12:1, 2. What are we encouraged to do?

_____

_____

_____

_____

_____

_____

GETTING IT RIGHT

Take a few moments to write down some of the trash that has been
piling up in the corners of your life lately. What do you think God wants
you to do with it? How do you think that trash smells to God?

_____

_____

_____

_____

_____

_____

_____

_____

_____

_____

_____

LIVING IT OUT

Look back at the list of things that you wrote down. Pick out one or
two that you will really concentrate on getting rid of during the next
few days. How will you do that?

_____

_____

_____

_____

_____

_____

_____

_____

_____

_____

TALKING TO GOD

As you are talking to God, ask him to help you throw off your sin, take out the trash and clean up your life.

_____

_____

_____

_____

_____

_____

_____

OTHER THOUGHTS

_____

_____

_____

_____

DAY 7 | BLANKET
God's protection

When I was a little kid, I worried about the monsters in my room. I would lie awake many nights in fear of them. There was one monster that lived in my closet. He could only come out at night if I left the closet door open. There was a laundry chute located in my closet that went down to the basement. Everyone knows that some of the the worst monsters come from the basement. So each night I'd make sure that my closet door was closed, to keep him from coming out and attacking me while I slept. But he wasn't the monster that I feared the most.

The worst, most treacherous and most powerful monster lived under my bed. He was a greenish color, with glowing red eyes and long tentacles that could snag any arm or leg that hung over the side of the bed during the night. The monster could reach out and wrap one of its tentacles around my ankle and drag me out of bed, onto the floor and under the bed where it would eat me for a midnight snack . . . Maybe I watched too much TV as a kid.

But there was one thing more powerful than all the monsters in my room. That one thing helped me sleep at night. That one thing saved me from a horrible death each and every night. That one thing was my blanket. There was something magical about my blanket—it formed a shield that no monster could penetrate. When I got into bed and turned the lights out, the monsters could prowl my room. But if I was in bed, tucked under my blanket, they couldn't touch me! As long as I was underneath that blanket, I could sleep like a baby.

Now that I'm older, I realize that I had an overactive imagination when I was growing up. But even though I don't worry about finding monsters in my room anymore, I still worry about a lot of things. I'm not like Charlie Brown's friend Linus any longer. I don't carry my blanket around all the time for protection and comfort, but I do rely on God's protection.

I wish that I had memorized Psalm 121 when I was a kid, hiding under my blanket for protection. A psalm is a very old poem or song that was written so that people could remember it and repeat it. This psalm tells me that God is my blanket of protection now and forever!

ENTERING IN

Read Psalm 121. How does it make you feel to think that God, who created everything, is ready to help you? Read Psalm 121 again and this time list all the things that God promised that he will do for us.

GETTING IT RIGHT

Look back at your list of promises that God gives us in Psalm 121. Pick out one or two that really jump out at you. What do you think God is trying to tell you or remind you of right now?

_____

_____

_____

_____

_____

_____

_____

_____

LIVING IT OUT

As you go through your day, keep a mental list of all the ways that God protects you. Some might be safety in travel, getting through a tough situation, whatever you can think of. Write some of these ways here.

_____

_____

_____

_____

_____

_____

TALKING TO GOD

Take a few moments to think about the times in the past when God has been your blanket of protection. Thank him for being there. Thank him for promising protection for you in future situations.

OTHER THOUGHTS

DAY 8 | PILLOWS
Standing firm

I don't know about you, but I used to love a good pillow fight. Occasionally my brother and I would square off against each other and beat each other with our pillows. But the biggest pillow fight of the year happened each fall when our youth group went on our retreat. Late at night all the boys in the dorm would grab their pillows for the annual "Guys-Only Pillow Fight Extravaganza!" We had a blast swinging away at twenty-five or thirty other guys. Fortunately there were no serious injuries!

I have to confess to you that I would always take an old pillow with me on those retreats. I had a healthy fear that my favorite pillow—I like my pillow to be thin and flat— would be ruined. Whenever I get a new one, it takes me some time to get it just the way I like it. I'll smash one edge down. I'll roll it up. I'll work it and work it until it's just perfect for me.

It may seem odd to focus on people's preferences in pillows, but think about it for minute. Is your favorite pillow thick or thin? Is it soft or hard? Is it made of down or artificial filler? No matter what kind of pillow you prefer, the purpose of a pillow is to be comfortable and help you sleep. A pillow conforms to your neck and head and makes it easier to start sawing logs.

The last time I stayed at a hotel, I slept horribly because the pillows were all wrong—huge, thick, almost round. I was dead tired, so I tried to go to sleep. It was no use; the pillow wouldn't conform to my head. It felt like I was trying to sleep on a basketball. After tossing and turning for what seemed like an eternity, I threw the pillow on the floor and ended up sleeping without a pillow for the rest of my stay.

Pillows are supposed to conform to our shape. But did you know that God doesn't want us to be like a pillow? Many times in the Bible, God tells us to go against the flow of popular opinion. He challenges us to be different from everyone else. He tells us not to do the accepted thing if it isn't right. Today we are going to be reading and thinking about God's challenge for us to be quite un-pillow-like.

ENTERING IN

Read Romans 12:1, 2. These verses challenge us not to be like fluffy pillows. What should we do with our bodies?

_____

_____

_____

_____

_____

What do the verses say about conforming?

_____

_____

_____

_____

GETTING IT RIGHT

Think about a couple of specific instances or areas in your life in which you feel squeezed to fit in. How do you feel when you conform instead of standing up for God? Write down one area in which you feel the pressure to go along with things you know aren't right.

_____

_____

_____

_____

_____

_____

_____

_____

_____

_____

LIVING IT OUT

I like how *The Message* paraphrases today's verses. It says, "Don't let the world squeeze you into its mold." As you go through your day, keep track of times and situations when you feel as though you are being squeezed to conform to what the world wants, and not what God wants.

_____

_____

_____

TALKING TO GOD

Have a conversation with God. Ask him to help you stand up and not conform. Ask him to give you the strength to not live a pillow-like life. Take a minute or two to ask him for help in the areas that are especially hard for you to stand firm in. Tell him anything you want him to know.

OTHER THOUGHTS

DAY 9 | CANDLES
Stinky attitudes

My parents made me wait until I was in high school before they allowed me to have candles in my room. They made me promise to be extremely careful with them so that I didn't burn down the house. One of my favorite things to do was to sit in my room and relax at the end of a long day. I'd light a couple of candles, listen to some good music and unwind.

There is something about the light from a candle that makes me feel at ease. I could stare at a candle and lose myself in my thoughts—I would usually wake up a few hours later and realize that I had dozed off!

For a candle to reach its full potential, it has to stay lit for a while. It's only after the wax begins to melt that the aroma can fill the room. It starts off as just a whiff, but over time it permeates the entire room. Sometimes the scent would seem faint to me, but if I left my room for a few minutes I would be overwhelmed by the pleasant smell when I returned. It smelled a lot better than my dirty soccer socks!

Candles come in a variety of scents. Some smell flowery or perfume-y. Others use the essence of fruits or oils. You can buy candles that smell like Grandma's apple pie, warm sugar cookies or hazelnut coffee. Even with all of these options, my favorite candle scent is good old vanilla.

I really enjoy a great-smelling candle. But there's nothing worse than one that smells like Grandma's bathroom spray! That got me wondering one day about what scent I would be if I were a candle. Would God like my aroma, or would he get one whiff of me and turn up his nose? Are my actions and attitudes pleasing to him, or is he repulsed by my hypocrisy?

Our lives can be described as an aroma. If you had to describe how your life smells to God, how would you describe it? Are you a pleasant smell, or do you smell like roses . . . rotten ones?

ENTERING IN

Read 2 Corinthians 2:14, 15. The text says that if we are Christians, we are spreading the fragrance of God. What do you think this means?

_____

_____

_____

_____

_____

_____

_____

Are you spreading a fragrance that is pleasing to God?

_____

_____

_____

_____

_____

_____

GETTING IT RIGHT

What actions or attitudes have you had in the last twenty-four hours that you would list as smelling good to God? What actions or attitudes have you had in the last twenty-four hours that God would say absolutely reek?

_____

_____

_____

_____

_____

_____

_____

LIVING IT OUT

As you go through today, keep track of your various actions and attitudes. Try to be a scent that is pleasing to God and not a disgusting odor.

_____

_____

_____

_____

_____

_____

TALKING TO GOD

Spend a few minutes asking God to forgive your stinky attitudes and actions. Also take time to review with him the positive parts of your day. Close out your conversation with God by asking God to help you improve the "smell" of your life.

_____

_____

_____

_____

_____

_____

_____

_____

_____

_____

_____

_____

OTHER THOUGHTS

_____

_____

_____

_____

DAY 10 | MAGAZINES
More to life

One *Saturday Evening_ I was too _Wired_ to relax, so I downloaded my _Playlist_ from my _PC_ onto my _Pocket PC_ and settled down to read some of my magazines. While I was listening to my favorite _Garage Band_, I picked up my sports periodical and got _Hooked_ on an article about a _Pro Football_ player who loved to _Ski_ and _Mountain Bike_ in the off-season as part of his training for the _Ironman_ competition. _Cycling_ and _Flexing_ put him in what he called the _Runner's World_. And it kept him from being the typical lazy _American Spectator_.

I then picked up another publication to _Find_ some _Trends_ for _Living_ in the _Ideal Home_. The more I read, the more I learned about how much _Money_ it takes to have one of the _Better Homes and Gardens_ in this _World_ and be considered to be living _The Good Life_.

Another journal had a _Feature_ article on _People_ who spend all their _Time Out_ in _Society_ amassing _Fortune_ and perceived _Worth_, while running with _Fast Company_. _U.S. News_ reported that a _National Review_ of _Atlantic_ travelers indicated that many _High Rollers_ preferred to vacation in the _Caribbean_, _Santa Barbara_, _Florida_ or _Cape Cod_. While on _Getaway_ they would spend a large chunk of their _Net Worth_ on _Food & Dining_, exotic _Spa_ treatments and enjoying the _Arts_.

I had had enough of this sort of thing, so I took a _Spin_ over to see what the _Word_ was in the _Men's World_. I'm more of a _Music_ and _Muscle Car_ kind of guy anyway. Give me some good old _American Iron_ or a sweet _Classic Car_ and I'm as _Fit_ as a fiddle. I get all the _Entertainment_ I need from a good _Film Premier_ or by checking out the _Trends_ in _Muscle Cars & Trucks_.

After a few hours of looking through sixteen or _Seventeen_ magazines, I realized that the _Allure_ of most of them was the _Glamour_ of great looks and the hottest _Fashion_. I asked myself, _Is there anything More? This can't be all there is for an American Girl, Modern Bride or Young Teen. There has got to be something Real that we can hold onto._

So I put down the magazines, picked up my Bible and found out that "_O_ yes," there is something _Genuine and Bone Fide_ that isn't marketed at newsstands. It's not found in a magazine. _Today's Reader_ can only discover how to live _Life_ to the fullest from studying God's Word, the Bible.

*Words that are underlined and italicized are actual magazine periodicals.

ENTERING IN

The life that magazines portray doesn't always match up with real life. You rarely see a picture of an ugly person in a magazine. The models are always beautiful or handsome and in great shape. Those who are interviewed always share about how great life is for them. They never seem to have any problems.

To be honest, my life isn't always pretty and things go wrong. Read James 4:13-17 to see what God has to say about what our expectations should be.

_____

_____

_____

_____

GETTING IT RIGHT

Does it surprise you that the writer of James comes on so strong?
How does it make you feel to know that you are not promised tomorrow
and that your life is like a mist that appears and then vanishes?

_____

_____

_____

_____

_____

_____

_____

_____

LIVING IT OUT

It is very easy for us to boast or brag about our accomplishments.
What is one thing that you take too much pride in? Is it your grades,
where you live, where you go to school, who you are dating?

_____

_____

_____

_____

_____

_____

_____

_____

Now reread today's verses. What is God trying to teach you through them? Carry that message with you.

_____

_____

TALKING TO GOD

Spend a few minutes thanking God for providing for you. Ask for forgiveness when you boast and brag about things that really don't matter. Tell him that you are sorry that you think that you control your life, and that you realize each day is a gift from him.

_____

_____

_____

_____

_____

_____

OTHER THOUGHTS

_____

_____

_____

_____

_____

DAY 11 | POSTERS
Windows of your soul

I remember that some of the biggest arguments my parents and I had were about the posters I wanted to hang on my walls. Being a guy, the posters I tried to hang in my room fell into three general categories: sports and music stars, hot girls and even hotter girls. If you are a girl, your posters probably fall into similar categories: hot guys, hot guys that are sports stars and hot guys that are music celebrities. My parents really didn't approve of most of the poster choices that I brought home, and they let me know it.

I wanted to have the walls of my room plastered with all the popular people that my friends and I thought were so cool. The problem was that behind the glamorous bodies and extravagant cars, many of them lived lives that were pretty bad. Most of the music and movie celebrities were known for making bad choices. Either they'd been in some kind of rehab program for drugs or alcohol, in the news for any number of violations or in and out of failed relationships. My parents knew that I would spend a lot of time in my room, looking at and thinking about those images. And most of the girls on the posters weren't exactly wearing their "Sunday best."

My mom and dad told me over and over again that the things that I looked at went into my mind. They told me that they wanted me to have positive role models who were really worth looking up to. They didn't want me to think of women as sex objects but as people. To be honest, I didn't really understand all that they were saying; I just knew that the approved poster selection probably would be limited to a skateboarder from the X-Games, a St. Louis Rams running back and a picture of Garfield saying, "Good Morning is an oxymoron."

It took me a long time to appreciate what my parents had been trying to teach me. My eyes are the windows to my soul. When I look at bad or negative things, it is easier to think bad or negative thoughts. Those bad images stay in my mind for a long time, and come flooding back all too often. But if I focus on good and positive things, I have a better chance of dwelling on good and positive thoughts.

ENTERING IN

My parents weren't the first people who knew that our eyes are the windows to our mind. Read about it in Matthew 6:22, 23. What does Jesus say?

_____

_____

_____

_____

_____

Read verse 21 too. How do you think this relates to the other two verses?

_____

_____

_____

_____

_____

GETTING IT RIGHT

What comes to your mind when you read these verses?

_____

_____

_____

_____

_____

_____

_____

_____

_____

_____

_____

Would you say that your body is more filled with light or darkness? Why?

_____

_____

_____

_____

_____

_____

_____

_____

LIVING IT OUT

Think about one poster, picture or person in your life that causes you to think bad thoughts. Write about this briefly in the space below.

Now that you have written it down, make a promise to God that you are going to try to avoid filling your eyes and mind with that image or thought.

_____

_____

_____

_____

_____

_____

_____

_____

Write here some positive thoughts or images that you can fill your mind with instead. Who are the people you know who are really worth looking up to?

_____

_____

_____

_____

_____

_____

_____

_____

_____

_____

TALKING TO GOD

Come clean before God about the things that are coming through your eyes and entering your mind. Ask him to help you eliminate the temptation to look at them and to erase the memory of them from your mind.

_____

_____

_____

_____

_____

_____

_____

_____

OTHER THOUGHTS

_____

_____

_____

_____

_____

_____

_____

_____

_____

DAY 12 | SPORTS EQUIPMENT
Using the full armor of God

I love sports. I tried to play about every sport that my school offered. And each time I went out for a new sport, I would need to get all the right equipment. Over the years I gathered quite a collection of balls, bats, shoes, pads and clothing. My room started to look more like a used sporting goods store than a bedroom.

My parents would comment on the huge amount of equipment I had in my room. I never got rid of any equipment that was still good enough to use—you never know when an extra batting glove will come in handy. You've got to have the right equipment for each sport. If you don't, a lot of things could go wrong. First of all, you'd be made fun of by the others on the team. "Hey, look at the guy with the hockey stick at tennis practice!" Can you imagine a soccer player running around with football shoulder pads on? What about a volleyball player wearing wrestling shoes? Or how funny would it be to see a swimmer dressed in a basketball uniform? Secondly, you wouldn't be able to compete very well. How would you be able to run the 100-yard dash for the track team in cleats? And thirdly, without the proper equipment, you could get hurt.

Having the right equipment makes a huge difference in the outcome of a game or a meet—but there's more to performing well than just having the right equipment. You have to know how to use the equipment. A baseball glove doesn't do any good if you never get to the ball. A tennis racquet won't help you lob the ball into your opponent's court if you don't make contact with the ball in the first place. A basketball won't find the hoop if you shoot like my sister.

Life is a lot like sports. You have to have the right equipment and know how to use it correctly to be successful in life. It's a good thing that God gives us some advice on how to handle our spiritual equipment.

ENTERING IN

Having the right equipment and knowing how to use it correctly is important in sports. It is also important in the Christian life. Read Ephesians 6:11-18 to learn about God's equipment. Who is our struggle against?

_____

_____

_____

_____

_____

_____

_____

List each piece of armor.

_____

_____

_____

_____

_____

GETTING IT RIGHT

What do you think God is trying to tell you from his Word today? Take a few minutes to evaluate how well you are using each piece of armor.

_____
_____
_____
_____
_____
_____
_____
_____
_____
_____
_____
_____

LIVING IT OUT

How can you use God's equipment, the armor of God, in your life right now?

_____
_____
_____
_____
_____
_____
_____
_____

What one piece of equipment stands out to you as one you know you need to have and use more effectively?

_____

_____

_____

_____

_____

TALKING TO GOD

Thank God for providing the right equipment for your spiritual life. Ask him to help you continue to improve in using each piece.

_____

_____

_____

_____

_____

_____

_____

OTHER THOUGHTS

_____

_____

_____

DAY 13 | COMPUTER
Seek and find

The odds are quite good that you have access to a computer—whether it's at home, at school, in a public library or at a cyber café. You may even be fortunate enough to have a computer in your room. Having a computer makes researching for homework or school projects easier. You can also play games, talk to your friends by e-mail or instant messaging and download music and videos. You can surf the Web and learn about anything in the world. The uses for computers, specifically those hooked up to the Internet, are potentially limitless. But in addition to all of the cool uses for computers, there are some equally bad and ugly ones.

A few months ago, I got together with a high school guy who used his computer to download pornographic pictures and videos. James was coming to me for help. He said that he felt as though he was addicted to the Internet and especially to pornography. James said that his parents had suspected that something was up when he spent hundreds of hours in his room online. They confronted him and had a Web blocker installed on his computer. But it took him all of about ten minutes to figure out how to get past the Web blocker, and then he was back to surfing the Internet whenever and wherever he wanted. In just a few minutes, James explained to me how easy it was for him to access awful pictures and videos. He even saved them on CD-ROMs so they would be available even if his parents cut off his Internet access.

James and I had a great discussion. He said that he had been thrilled when his parents first got him the computer and a cable modem for Internet access. He loved online games and being able to check out his favorite artists' newest songs. He even planned to use it for research and school projects. But he had turned something good into a monster that was controlling his life. James was ready to change because he realized that the computer was taking over his life and that God was no longer in control.

I'm thankful that James found some help and that his family made some valuable changes. They moved his computer from his room to a central location in the house. James even went back to dial-up for six months so that his Internet access was severely limited and downloads were painfully slow. It took a long time, but James eventually got to the point where he could use his computer again for the good that was intended and avoid the lure of temptation.

ENTERING IN

Read Proverbs 11:27. This verse talks about two different kinds of seekers. One seeks good and the other seeks evil. Make a list of areas in which you seek good and evil.

Good: _____

_____

_____

_____

Evil: _____

_____

_____

_____

GETTING IT RIGHT

Looking at the lists you made, how do you feel about the ones listed as good? How does it make you feel when you use your mind and talents to do good things?

_____

_____

_____

_____

_____

_____

_____

_____

_____

_____

_____

_____

_____

Now focus on the things listed under the evil heading. How does it make you feel when you see those things listed? The reality is that it took a lot of courage for you to write them down on this page. This verse contains a promise for us—that if we search after evil things, we will find them.

_____

_____

_____

_____

_____

_____

_____

_____

_____

_____

_____

_____

Most of the time we think that we can escape the consequences of the bad things we do. We think, *I'll never get caught. It couldn't happen to me.* The truth is that we will face the bad consequences, and they are the fulfillment of this promise. Write about one time when you had to face the consequences of your bad actions. How did you feel?

_____

_____

_____

_____

_____

_____

_____

_____

_____

LIVING IT OUT

It's time to get serious about searching after good and not wasting our time searching after evil things. There is also a promise for us if we seek after good things—we'll find them.

Now that you know what bad or evil things you search after, remind yourself—every time that you are tempted to search after evil—that God promises you'll find it. Where can you look to find more good things?

_____

_____

_____

_____

_____

_____

_____

_____

_____

_____

_____

_____

_____

_____

_____

_____

TALKING TO GOD

Wrap up this quiet time by asking God to give you the strength not to search after evil, but only after good. Maybe you feel trapped, like James did, and you need to talk to someone. Ask God to give you the courage to find someone you can share your struggle with and begin to escape from it.

OTHER THOUGHTS

DAY 14 | PICTURE FRAMES
A different kind of love

I f you are like me, pictures are important to you. Maybe you don't take a ton of photos, but I'm guessing that you probably have at least one picture of your friends somewhere in your room. Maybe it's up on your wall or on top of your dresser. Maybe it's a snapshot from a photo booth or a picture that was e-mailed to you. Maybe you've taken the time to put your favorite picture into an album or a frame.

I have a framed picture of two very special friends of mine who go to church with me. Their names are Tina and Macie. Tina is in her thirties and Macie is her niece. Since Tina isn't married and doesn't have any kids of her own, she and Macie have developed a really special relationship. They love to spend time together and do a lot of "girl stuff."

It may seem kind of odd that I keep their photo up, but there's more to the story than just their friendship. A couple of years ago, Macie started having some health problems. At first the doctors didn't know what was wrong with Macie, but after a series of tests, they determined that Macie had a rare disease that was attacking her kidneys. Over the next few months, Macie spent more time in the hospital getting treatments than she did out of the hospital. She missed so much school that she had to repeat a grade. It seemed that nothing the doctors tried was doing any good. She just kept getting sicker and sicker and weaker and weaker.

Finally the doctors came to Macie's parents with some bad news. They told her parents that unless Macie could get a new kidney, she would never get any better. Fortunately, there was a way for Macie's family and friends to get tested to see if they could donate a kidney to her. As it turned out they did find a match. The perfect donor was her Aunt Tina. When Macie and her parents found out, they approached Tina and told her that she was a perfect match. Then Macie asked her aunt if she would be willing to donate one of her kidneys to her. Without hesitation Tina said that she would do anything she could to save Macie's life.

I wish I could say that the kidney transplant was an easy procedure, but it wasn't. There was a fear that Macie's body would reject the new organ, so she had to take a lot of pills to prevent that. And Tina's recovery turned out to be much harder than Macie's. For some reason the person donating her kidney usually has a harder time healing from the surgery than the person getting the new kidney.

But after many months, they were both together again, laughing and having fun. I took their picture at a youth event at our church and framed it. Tina's willingness to risk her life for someone she loved really made an impression on me. In fact, that picture reminds me that there is someone who loves us so much that he gave up his life for me . . . and for you.

ENTERING IN

Read John 15:12, 13. These verses say that we are to love one another and that the greatest way we could show our love is to lay down our lives for a friend. How does that concept make you feel?

GETTING IT RIGHT

Who do you think would give up his life for you if it meant saving your life? Why?

_____

_____

_____

_____

_____

_____

_____

_____

_____

Is there anyone in your life that you would be willing to sacrifice your life for, if it meant that that person could live? Why or why not?

_____

_____

_____

_____

_____

_____

_____

_____

_____

LIVING IT OUT

The first part of our Scripture challenges us to love one another. Write down two people's names and one way that you can show that you love each one of them.

_____

_____

_____

_____

_____

_____

_____

_____

_____

If there is someone in your life that you feel would lay down her life for you, find an opportunity to thank that person for loving you so much. What could you do to say thanks?

_____

_____

_____

_____

_____

_____

_____

_____

Whether you believe it or not, someone has given up his life for you already. His name is Jesus. How does that make you feel?

_____

_____

_____

_____

_____

_____

_____

_____

Why do you think Jesus loves you enough to sacrifice everything for you?

_____

_____

_____

_____

_____

_____

_____

_____

_____

_____

_____

TALKING TO GOD

Spend some time thanking Jesus for loving you enough to die on the cross for you. Think about what kind of love that is and how it should affect you.

_____

_____

_____

_____

_____

_____

_____

_____

_____

OTHER THOUGHTS

_____

_____

_____

_____

_____

_____

_____

_____

_____

DAY 15 | DIRTY CLOTHES
Coming clean

There are basically two types of people in the world when it comes to handling dirty clothes. The first group puts them into the hamper or down the dirty clothes chute as soon as they take them off. These are the people who think that dirty clothes are gross and need to be cleaned as soon as possible. The second type—mostly guys—views dirty clothes as a way to protect the carpet from getting worn out too quickly. If the clothes aren't too bad, they give them a quick shot of spray deodorant and wear them two or three more times or until they walk away on their own. This type of person drops the clothes on the floor and doesn't worry about picking them up until threatened with severe punishment or until a science project evolves from the chaos.

I'm more like the second group of people. For a while I just didn't feel like picking up my dirty clothes anymore. It might have worked out OK if it hadn't happened at the same time my mom decided that it was time for me to learn to be more responsible. She informed me that I didn't have to pick up my clothes anymore but that she wasn't going to either. I was thrilled—no more cleaning up dirty clothes!

I remember wearing the same clothes—to school, to play, to ball practice—virtually everywhere. When they finally reached the point that it was inconsiderate to wear them in public, I'd pile them at the end of my bed. After a couple of weeks, it started to smell really bad in my room.

I knew that it was getting bad when one of my friends asked me if my dad had lost his job and we didn't have enough money to wash the clothes. I had worn my favorite pair of jeans for five straight days!

I eventually gave in and picked up my room. I had learned to appreciate having clothes that didn't look like they'd been stuffed in a garbage can for a week. I finally realized that picking up my dirty clothes was a small price to pay for keeping my mom happy and having clean clothes.

ENTERING IN

Read Isaiah 64:5, 6. What do these verses mean to you?

_____

_____

_____

_____

_____

_____

_____

This Scripture says that when we live without God, even the good things that we do are like yesterday's laundry. Have you ever thought of yourself as being like dirty laundry?

_____

_____

_____

_____

_____

_____

_____

GETTING IT RIGHT

What do you think God is trying to tell you through his Word today?

_____

_____

_____

_____

_____

_____

_____

_____

LIVING IT OUT

How have your actions been like dirty clothes toward God?

_____

_____

_____

_____

_____

_____

What can you do to clean up your dirty laundry?

_____

_____

_____

TALKING TO GOD

Spend a couple of minutes talking to God about the dirty laundry in your life. Go ahead and be specific. You don't have anything to hide because he already knows everything about you. Ask God for his help in cleaning up the problem areas in your life.

OTHER THOUGHTS

Solid foundation

M y brother Kevin and I loved to play board games
together. I would go to his room, or he'd come to
mine, and we'd have these huge competitions in
which we'd play a game, and the loser had to do one chore
for the winner the next week. The only consolation was that
the loser got to choose which game we played next. We
competed over Monopoly®, Sorry®, Rock-em Sock-em®;
Robots®, Battleship® and many others. But one game was
our all-time favorite—Stratego®!

Stratego® is basically the board game version of "Capture
the Flag." Each team has fourteen scouts and miners, eight
high-ranking soldiers, one marshal, one colonel and six bombs
which blow up everything—excluding the miners—and one
flag. The object of the game is to capture the opponent's flag
while avoiding the bombs and protecting your own flag. The
person who captures the other person's flag first, wins. The
loser has to collect the garbage or do the dishes for a week.

My brother usually hid his flag in one of the back corners
surrounded by bombs and high-ranking officers. I liked to be a
little more adventurous and a bit sneakier. I usually put a bunch
of bombs and officers in one of the back corners just like he
did. But I rarely hid my flag there. Often I would hide my flag in
the middle of all the soldiers, or I might put it in the front line
behind a lake. My brother nearly always fell for the trap, so
unless something went drastically wrong, I would be the victor.

When I won I would do some sort of victory dance and make
up a chant that usually included the chore he had to do for
me. And then my brother would do something that bugged the
heck out of me. He'd lift up the board, dump the remaining

pieces into the box, fold up the board, and put the game back into the closet. I always felt ripped off. I mean, I was just getting into my victory dance and he was walking out of the room. What was the deal?! I had worked hard for that victory, and it was over just like that? Wow!

I soon figured out that life is a lot like a board game. I work and work. I practice and practice. I plan and plan. And when I win—it's over. Things that I put a lot of time and effort into turn out to be short-lived. It's almost like they don't mean anything at all. They're quickly forgotten and replaced by something else. It's taken me a while to figure out which things are really important and worth the effort. If you've ever felt a bit empty after having achieved something you thought would be a major accomplishment, you're definitely not alone.

Jesus talked about having the right priorities in our lives, but he didn't use a board game as an illustration. Read on to find out what story he told.

ENTERING IN

Read Matthew 7:24-29. Jesus talked about two guys who were building their dream houses. One did it right and built on a rock foundation. The other guy got in a hurry and built his on the sand—his victory was short-lived.

GETTING IT RIGHT

What was Jesus trying to tell us about building on the right things?

_____

_____

_____

_____

If you were a building inspector, would you say that your life is being built on a rock-solid or a shifting-sand foundation?

_____

_____

_____

_____

_____

_____

_____

LIVING IT OUT

How do you think you can build your life on God's strong foundation more effectively? Think about one area in your life and write it down here.

_____

_____

_____

_____
_____
_____
_____
_____
_____
_____
_____

TALKING TO GOD

Spend some time asking God to help you build your life with him as your strong foundation.

_____
_____
_____
_____
_____
_____
_____
_____

OTHER THOUGHTS

_____
_____
_____

DAY 17 | JOURNAL
Being real with God

My little sister kept a diary in her room. My brother and I loved to sneak into her room and read through her diary. Then some time later we'd make snide comments or ask about a boy that she had written about. She would instantly know that we had been snooping in her private diary again. And boy, did she get mad! Maybe we were the reason she stopped writing in her diary.

These days, diaries have been replaced by journals. I keep three journals, and each one has a specific purpose. There is my leather speaker journal. It's the one that I take notes in whenever I hear someone speak about a topic that I want to learn more about. I also have an idea journal, which I keep in a drawer close by. Whenever an idea hits me, I grab a pen and jot it down. But the journal that means the most to me is my spiritual journal.

I use my spiritual journal at night before I go to bed. Each night I write down my thoughts from the day, and I take some time to thank God for loving my family and me. I try to write out the things that I did that were wrong or things that I said that were untrue or that hurt others. I wrap up my spiritual journaling by asking God to work in certain situations. Maybe I know someone who is sick, or who is going through a tough time. No matter how big or small the situation, I write it down and ask for God's help.

Journaling helps me stay focused when I'm talking to God. If I just sit in bed and pray, my mind tends to wander. And yes, sometimes I fall asleep. But journaling keeps me focused. I can think through what I'm saying to God as I'm writing it down. I also love to flip back and look at the situations that I asked

God to work in. When I look back it's easy to see how God is working. I have to admit that when I am just praying and not journaling, I tend to forget what I've asked for and also that God answers my prayers.

If you were to read my journal—which I hope you never do—you would read some of my deepest and most private thoughts. You'd see the things that I've asked God for. You'd get to read about the best and even the worst experiences of my life. You'd see how God has carried me through the hard times that I've faced.

God is the best confidant available. And unlike snoopy little brothers, he doesn't have to slip into your room and sneak a peek at your life journal. God knows everything about you—whether you write it in a journal or not. He knew you before you were born. He knows everything that you are going to do in life. Even so, he loves it when we invite him to be part of the thoughts and experiences we treasure most.

ENTERING IN

Read Psalm 139:1-4, 13-18 and 23, 24. Isn't it great to know that you are in God's journal? How does it feel to know that God has loved you since before you were born?

_____

_____

_____

_____

_____

How does it feel to have God know you better than you know yourself?

_____

_____

_____

_____

_____

_____

_____

_____

GETTING IT RIGHT

Verses 1-4 talk about God knowing our every move and every thought. Is that a good thing or a bad thing for you? Why or why not?

_____

_____

_____

_____

_____

_____

_____

_____

What is the one action you are most ashamed of that God knows you've done in the past?

_____

_____

_____

_____

_____

_____

_____

_____

_____

What do you struggle with that you would rather God not know about?

_____

_____

_____

_____

_____

_____

_____

_____

_____

What is one action or attitude that you know God is proud of you for?

_____

_____

_____

_____

_____

_____

_____

_____

LIVING IT OUT

Pick one action phrase from today's text and write it here. Carry this action phrase with you all day and do what it says whenever you get the chance.

_____

_____

_____

_____

_____

_____

_____

_____

_____

TALKING TO GOD

Sometimes it can be pretty tough to know what to say to God. How do you talk to someone who knows you better than you do yourself? Try reading verses 23 and 24 as a prayer to him.

_____

_____

_____

_____

_____

_____

_____

OTHER THOUGHTS

_____

_____

_____

_____

_____

_____

_____

_____

_____

_____

DAY 18 | AUTOGRAPHS
To know you

For some reason, our society seems to value the autographs of famous people. Whether it's an athlete, a politician, a movie celebrity or a music star, we want their signature. We'll stand in line for hours for a mere chance to catch a glimpse of our heroes. One time I was over at my friend's house and he was telling a story about his friend Ozzie Smith. Ozzie Smith, known as "The Wizard of Oz," was an incredible athlete and is described by many as one of baseball's greatest defensive shortstops of all time. He won thirteen Gold Glove Awards in nineteen seasons with the Padres and Cardinals. Ozzie finished his career with over 2,400 hits and 500 stolen bases.

I found it hard to believe that my friend actually knew Ozzie Smith, so I questioned him on their relationship. I said, "You know Ozzie Smith? Really? Prove it to me."

So my friend walked over to the bookshelf in his bedroom and said, "Here, this proves it!" He handed me a framed picture that had Ozzie's signature and "#1" on it.

When I said, "OK, you've got his autograph, but do you know him?" my friend got a funny look on his face.

"Well," he said, "When I asked him for an autograph he said 'Sure' so I guess you could say we know each other."

I couldn't believe that my friend actually thought that he really knew Ozzie Smith. "You don't know Ozzie! He's not your friend! You just have his autograph! He wouldn't even recognize you if you introduced yourself to him again!"

"I guess you're right, but at least I've got his autograph," my friend finally relented, as he took back Ozzie's autograph.

Sometimes we confuse an autograph and a brief encounter with actually knowing someone—it makes us feel good to believe that we have a relationship with someone important. I think that the same thing happens with our relationship with God. We claim to know him and have a relationship with him, but the reality is that we have spent very little time getting to know him. The really cool thing is that, unlike most famous people, God really does want to know us. He always wants to spend time with us, hear what's going on in our lives, and be part of everything we experience. God has given us the Bible—his autograph book—so that we can know him, his character and his love for us.

ENTERING IN

We all know a lot of people. We have class with them, eat lunch with them, play sports with them and hang out with them. It's easy to find ways to get to know people, but how can we know God? Read 1 John 4:8 and find one of the ways that we can know God better.

GETTING IT RIGHT

Today's verse says that to know God we must love others. What comes to your mind when you think of loving others? Is there a name or a person's face that you think of?

_____

_____

_____

_____

_____

_____

_____

_____

_____

_____

_____

LIVING IT OUT

Write down one way that you can show love to others more fully.

_____

_____

_____

_____

_____

_____

TALKING TO GOD

Take a few minutes to ask God to help you love others more fully.

_____

_____

_____

_____

_____

_____

_____

_____

_____

_____

_____

_____

_____

_____

_____

_____

OTHER THOUGHTS

_____

_____

_____

_____

CARPET
Looking good on the surface

hen I was in high school, our family moved to another house in town. I was excited because I finally had my own bedroom. I loved everything about my room—except the carpet. The carpet was older than my grandmother and worn out, with several nasty stains on it.

Thankfully, a few weeks after we moved in, my parents had new carpet installed in my room. I was there when the carpet installers pulled out the old carpet. I was amazed at how much dirt was under the old rug! We had vacuumed the carpet several times, but there was still a layer of dirt under the carpet that the guys had to sweep up and then vacuum before they could lay the new carpet.

I have to admit that even though we had only lived there a short time, I was a little embarrassed and grossed out. I asked the guys if they always found this much dirt under old carpet and they said that what they found under my carpet wasn't that bad. They told me of one house where they had to use shovels to remove all the dirt! Then they explained that dirt settles down through the carpet and gathers under it. Even when you vacuum a carpet, some dirt always finds its way down to the floor. They said that even the best-looking carpet has some dirt underneath it.

That got me thinking about how people can hide stuff just like a carpet hides dirt. In particular, I started thinking about my friend Phil. We played ball together, and our families knew each other pretty well. Phil and his family always seemed really happy, until one day Phil surprised me by telling me that his parents were getting a divorce. I couldn't believe it!

Then Phil told me that his dad had always had a problem with alcohol. A couple of months before, the company his dad worked for had had to lay some people off, and his dad lost his job. Phil said that his dad began to drink more and more. He said that his dad would come home late at night after being out drinking, and Phil would pretend to be asleep in his bed so that his dad wouldn't come into his room and yell at him. Finally his mom couldn't take it anymore, and she filed for divorce.

I was shocked. Phil's family looked so good on the outside, but deep down they were having major problems. It was kind of like the dirt hidden under that old carpet.

I started to think about myself a little bit then. On the outside I can look like everything is going great—even if I'm struggling on the inside. I am pretty good at putting on a mask to make myself look a whole lot better than I really am. But I know that's not pleasing to Jesus. In Matthew 23 Jesus talked about being a hypocrite and appearing to be clean, but actually being really messed up on the inside.

ENTERING IN

Can you think of a time when you acted like you had it all together, but you were really hiding pain, hurt, embarrassment or some other junk? Today's text shows us what Jesus said about people who appear to be perfect but actually are pretty nasty inside. Read Matthew 23:25–28.

GETTING IT RIGHT

What do you think Jesus meant when he said that the Pharisees and teachers were like whitewashed tombs that look beautiful on the outside but are filled with dead people's bones on the inside?

Think about ways that you have faked how good you are or put yourself in a better light to those around you this week. Jot them down here.

What is some of the dirt that you have hidden under your carpet?

_____

_____

_____

_____

_____

_____

_____

_____

_____

LIVING IT OUT

We get really good at faking how great life is, when on the inside we are crying out for help. Why do you ever put on a fake face?

_____

_____

_____

_____

_____

_____

_____

What could you do instead of faking?

_____

_____

_____

_____

_____

_____

_____

_____

Focus on the hidden dirt that you are carrying around in your life. Then pick out one trusted friend or adult that you can talk to about what you are hiding.

_____

_____

_____

_____

_____

_____

_____

_____

_____

_____

TALKING TO GOD

Spend some time talking to God about the things you've hidden under your carpet. Thank God that he loves us no matter what's under our carpet. Then ask God to help you be honest about who you really are.

_____

_____

_____

_____

_____

_____

_____

_____

OTHER THOUGHTS

_____

_____

_____

_____

_____

_____

_____

_____

DAY 20 | PETS
Real relationships

I grew up in a home where pets did not belong inside the house. My dog and my sister's cats lived in the garage. I had a golden retriever named Teddy. That may seem like a silly name for a female, but I named her that because she was fluffy like a teddy bear. I loved to spend time with Teddy—we did everything together. When I rode my bike around the neighborhood, she'd follow along. When I played baseball down at the school, she'd join us. We even went through obedience school together—for the dog, not me! She learned how to heel, sit, stay, fetch, roll over and play dead. I loved that dog.

Teddy didn't just like to be outside; she didn't know anything different because our family had a strict rule that pets stay out at all times. But one winter a severe storm came through and the temperatures dropped below zero. The people on the news were warning pet owners to bring their pets inside as they could freeze to death if they were left in the cold. My sister and I begged our parents to let us bring in the cats and Teddy. They finally relented, and we went out and got them.

Since our pets weren't used to being in the house, we put them in our bedrooms and closed the doors. We were trying to keep them from running wild through the house and to minimize the area for potential "accidents." I was so excited that I spent the whole evening in my room playing with Teddy.

When it was time to go to bed, Teddy slept at my feet, keeping them warm all night long. I remember thinking about the saying that a dog is man's best friend. I agreed that Teddy was my best friend and companion.

Then one summer morning my friendship with Teddy came to an end. She hadn't been acting normal for a couple of days. She just stayed in her doghouse and refused to eat. That morning she didn't come out to greet me like she normally did. I went over to her house and discovered that Teddy had died during the night.

I missed Teddy. If you've ever lost a pet, you know how I felt. She was the most loyal friend I had ever had, and it was hard to let her go. I have lost other pets and good friends since Teddy, and each time that happens I have a better understanding of just how much I need relationships.

ENTERING IN

It's hard when a favorite pet dies. It is even harder when a person that we know and love dies. Why does it hurt? It hurts because we love them. Friends care for us in the good and bad times. They have our back when we need their support. Read Proverbs 17:17. What does this verse have to say about friends?

_____

_____

_____

_____

_____

_____

_____

_____

_____

GETTING IT RIGHT

Write down the name of a friend that you could call on at any time and he would come and help you out.

_____

_____

Can you think of a time when a friend really needed you and you helped her? How did it feel to stick close?

_____

_____

_____

_____

_____

_____

_____

LIVING IT OUT

Our pets know that we love them, because we take care of them. People are a little different from our pets. We need to tell them that we care for them. Think about your best friend. Sometime today take the time to tell your friend how much you value your friendship. You can talk face-to-face, write a note, call or send an e-mail. But do it. Don't wait until it's too late. Write here what you want to say.

_____

_____

_____

_____

_____

_____

_____

TALKING TO GOD

Spend a few moments thanking God for your good friends. Ask him to help you be available whenever one of your friends needs your help. Thank God for being your closest friend.

If you have some extra time, read Proverbs 18:24.

_____

_____

_____

_____

_____

_____

_____

OTHER THOUGHTS

_____

_____

_____

DAY 21 | T-SHIRTS
God's advertising

G rowing up, I had quite a collection of t-shirts. It seemed that whenever I or someone in my family would travel anywhere, I'd get a t-shirt. The time that my grandparents went to the Grand Canyon, they bought me one that read, "My grandparents went to the Grand Canyon and all I got was this t-shirt." I also got ones from them from Niagara Falls, Disney World and Dallas, Texas.

Now, it wasn't just my grandparents who gave me t-shirts. I got t-shirts from my school, my soccer team, my parents and my youth group. And I have to admit, I bought many for myself as well. It seemed that whatever I did, I got a t-shirt. I accumulated a lot of t-shirts this way.

I would keep my t-shirts folded in a drawer in my dresser. My mom complained that she was having a hard time fitting them in there when she put away my clean clothes. She encouraged me to take a look at them and get rid of the ones that I didn't wear anymore.

This turned out to be a tougher job than I anticipated for several reasons. First of all, I liked all of them, and it was hard to decide which ones to keep and which ones to get rid of. Second, I felt bad about getting rid of something that someone had given me as a gift. I mean, what would I do if they asked about the shirt and I'd thrown it away? The third reason was the biggest—I had a lot of t-shirts. When I pulled them all out of the drawer and counted them I had—are you ready for this?—ninety-two t-shirts! Can you believe it!

As I worked through the shirts, it became clear to me that each shirt was advertising something different. It might be a vacation spot, a school mascot, a church retreat or whatever. The message was clear. When you wear the t-shirt, you advertise what's printed on it. It caused me to think about my life as a Christian.

If you think about it, you are a walking advertisement for God. What that looks like depends on you and your life. If you do your best to live for God, for the most part, you will be a positive advertisement for him. But if you are constantly messing up and doing the wrong things you will be a negative one. When people look at you, what is their perception of God? Do they see someone who is trying to do what is right or someone who is trying to see what they can get away with?

ENTERING IN

Today you are going to read and learn that what we do does reflect on God. Read Ephesians 5:11-15, 18-21.

In these verses Paul says that we are ambassadors for Christ. An ambassador is someone who represents someone or something else.

_____

_____

_____

_____

_____

_____

_____

_____

GETTING IT RIGHT

Have you ever thought of your life as a t-shirt advertising God before? If you could design a shirt that represented how people see God in you, what would it look like?

_____

_____

_____

_____

_____

_____

_____

LIVING IT OUT

Whether you realize it or not, if you are a Christian, people are watching you to see what being a Christian looks like. They want to see if it is worth it or not. Sometimes that is a heavy burden, but being a follower of Christ isn't always easy.

How do you want others to see God through you? Make a list of ways that you can try to make that happen.

_____

_____

_____

_____

_____

_____

_____

_____

_____

_____

_____

TALKING TO GOD

Being an ambassador for Christ may seem overwhelming at times. It may seem unfair on other occasions. But the truth is, the way that we live out our faith might be the only Christian example some of our friends see.

Spend a few minutes asking God to help you live your life so that people can get a clear picture of him.

_____

_____

_____

_____

_____

OTHER THOUGHTS

_____

_____

_____

_____

22 | BIBLE
To know him better

What place does your Bible have in your room? Do you keep your Bible in one place so that you can grab it each day when you have your quiet time? Or do you treat your Bible like it's insignificant? Do you come home from church or youth group and toss your Bible on the floor or onto your desk, like dirty clothes that get taken off and thrown in a pile or kicked toward the hamper? How many times has the rest of your family waited for you in the car before church while you were in your room frantically searching for your Bible? The way that you treat your Bible is usually a good indicator of the depth of your relationship with God.

I don't know about you, but I want to know God's will for my life. There have been many times when I have asked God, "What should I do? Which direction should I go in my life?" I would love it if God would speak to me or give me a sign. That has never happened for me, but God has given me all that I need to know to get through life and go to Heaven—it's all in the Bible. The Bible can answer our questions and give us the direction we need for our lives.

This truth came to life for me in high school. I was going out with Jessica, and I was head-over-heels in love with her. We had been dating for a while when I felt that she was pulling away from the relationship. She started hanging out with her friends more and more and confiding in others instead of me. One night I was driving my best friend Ben to a ball game at school. I shared with him what I was thinking and feeling. Ben sat quietly for a moment then he shared with me that he and Jessica had been seeing each other for a while and she wanted to end it with me!

I couldn't believe it! My best friend was hooking up with my girlfriend? I dropped Ben off at school and went home to find refuge in my room. While I was in my room, I moved from feeling incredibly hurt to having extreme anger toward both of them. I wanted to get back at them in a big way!

For some reason, I picked up my Bible and turned to Romans 12:19, 20. As I read it, it told me that it's God's job to repay evil for evil, and it's my job to forgive. Wow! That is hard to do.

There's a part of me that would like to tell you that Ben and Jessica were struck by lightning the next day, but that didn't happen. I did, however, eventually forgive them—once I realized that paybacks are God's department and not mine.

ENTERING IN

Read Romans 12:19, 20. Have you ever read something in the Bible that you thought was really hard to believe or follow? What was it?

GETTING IT RIGHT

Think about a situation when you didn't know what to do and wanted to get advice from someone. Who did you go to? Why?

_____

_____

_____

_____

_____

_____

_____

_____

_____

Did you turn to God as well? Did you look to the Bible for help? Why or why not?

_____

_____

_____

_____

_____

_____

_____

_____

_____

_____

If one of the major ways that God communicates his direction for our life is through the Bible, why don't you study it more to find his will? List all of your reasons below.

_____

_____

_____

_____

_____

_____

_____

Today's verses challenge us to leave vengeance in God's hands. How can you do that today?

_____

_____

_____

_____

_____

_____

_____

_____

_____

_____

We are to repay evil with good—that's really tough. How can you show kindness in a situation in which you've been wronged?

_____

_____

_____

_____

_____

_____

_____

_____

_____

LIVING IT OUT

It seems pretty simple. God gave us the Bible so we can know him better and know how to make wise decisions in our lives. The obvious fact is that we need to study and live by the guidelines in the Bible. But we need to read the Bible to know those guidelines.

Make a commitment to reach a goal of reading the Bible at least three times a week—outside of church—so that you can know God's will for your life. Write your promise here.

_____

_____

_____

_____

TALKING TO GOD

If you aren't taking advantage of God's Word and are relying on your own judgment, realize that you will make a lot of mistakes. Take some time to ask for forgiveness for not utilizing one of the best tools we've been given. Then ask God to give you the strength to dive into his Word on a regular basis.

OTHER THOUGHTS

DAY 23 | DESK
Life's real purpose

've never liked math. My dislike for math has more than a little to do with the fact that I've never been good at it. And that was made worse by the fact that my mom taught . . . math! Not only did she teach math, she loved math.

I managed to keep my extreme dislike for math to myself until variables were introduced in Algebra. I must have been absent on the day in Algebra class that the teacher told us what x equals. From that day on, I was confused. My teacher kept saying that x was the unknown number—that couldn't have been truer for me. By the time that midterm grades had been averaged, my grade had sunk to a D.

My parents were more than a bit concerned about my grades and were certain that I could do better in Algebra. In an effort to remove me from some of the distractions of studying in the living room, they got a desk for me and moved it into my room. It wasn't very big, but I put a lamp and a small shelf for some books on it, and I filled the drawer with pencils, pens and supplies that I'd need to do my homework. This wooden desk became the epicenter for all of my homework. When I got home from school, I'd head straight upstairs and sit at my desk to do my homework.

I'll never forget the hours I spent studying for midterms and final exams, but one of my favorite memories of working at that desk is from my freshman science project. I was study-ing the effects that occur when various substances are mixed together. The experiment was supposed to be simple: observe how baking soda and vinegar expand when they are mixed. So I poured some of each into a bottle and put a balloon over the mouth of the bottle. What happened was spectacular! The balloon expanded so much that it flew off the bottle, knocking it over. The pressure from the reaction caused the bottle to spin, spewing white foam all over the desk, wall, floor and myself! After I cleaned up the mess, I got an A on that project.

I have to admit that my study did improve when I sat at my desk and concentrated, but I'd be lying to you if I told you that I got straight As in high school. It's a good thing for me that my parents had realistic expectations for my grades. Of course they wanted me to do well in school and give my best effort, but they also knew that I was created for more than schoolwork. They encouraged me to play soccer and try different forms of art while I was in school. Most importantly, they encouraged me to pursue a relationship with God.

The Bible says that having a relationship with God is more important than amassing knowledge. Are you giving as much effort to your relationship with God as to your grades? friendships? sports? hobbies? Make sure that you're giving God the priority he deserves!

ENTERING IN

If we let ourselves lose focus on what is really important, we set ourselves up for a fall when things don't work out the way that we want. The wisest man ever to live, King Solomon, found this out the hard way. But he also discovered the real purpose of life. Check it out in Ecclesiastes 12:12, 13.

GETTING IT RIGHT

According to the verses you just read, what are the two secrets to knowing the meaning of life?

_____

_____

_____

_____

_____

_____

_____

_____

What grade would you give yourself on knowing each one of them? Why?

_____

_____

_____

_____

_____

_____

_____

_____

_____

_____

_____

_____

What would you say that you have been striving after in life? Grades, friendships, good behavior, popularity, sports? Write down a couple of things and say why you strive after them .

_____

_____

_____

_____

_____

_____

_____

_____

_____

_____

LIVING IT OUT

As you look over the things that you just wrote down, how do they measure up to Solomon's advice?

_____

_____

_____

_____

_____

_____

Fearing God means respecting him and obeying his commands. Choose one of his commands that you are not obeying—whether you're all-out disobeying or just slacking—and make it your number one priority today to obey that command in all you do, say and think. Write the command here.

How can you avoid disobeying this command in particular?

TALKING TO GOD

Spend a few minutes talking to God. Thank him for the wisdom he gave Solomon and for bringing his words to your attention today. Then ask him to help you fear and obey him, especially in the areas you have decided to concentrate on today.

OTHER THOUGHTS

DAY 24 | CHAIR
Intentional relationships

I used to have a chair at the desk in my room—but it was more than just a chair. My family had it for many years, and I'm not sure where it came from. There was nothing spectacular about it, but I used that chair for everything.

At times the chair was a clothes rack. When I came home from school I was always in such a hurry to change into more comfortable clothes that I didn't want to take the time to throw the dirty clothes down the laundry chute. So I would toss my clothes onto the back of the chair. I would also hang my jacket over the back so that I could grab it quickly on my way out.

I often used the chair like a step stool or ladder. When I needed to reach a high shelf or change a light bulb in the ceiling fixture, it was much faster to use the chair than to find a stepladder and drag it up to my room.

That chair was also a shelf. I put my football helmet on it when I wasn't using it. And anytime I was working on a project, I used the chair to hold it.

During high school the chair doubled as a piece of workout equipment. I would put my feet on the chair and my hands on the ground to do inverted push-ups. Then I'd turn over and put my legs on the chair and do hard crunches. When I wasn't working out on the chair, I put my keys, wallet and watch on it at night, so I could always find them when I got ready for school in the morning.

And yes, I actually used the chair for its intended purpose. I would sit in it at my desk to do my homework, read a book, do research for papers and use the computer.

It's kind of amazing that a simple wooden chair could be so versatile and help me do so many things. I can't think of anything else that I had in my room that I used for that many different things. I had just never stopped to think about all the uses for a simple wooden chair. In a way our relationships with God are supposed to be like my chair—versatile.

ENTERING IN

Check out 1 Corinthians 9:19-23. This passage could seem a little confusing at first, but it all comes together in verse 22. What does that verse say?

_____

_____

_____

_____

_____

Paul writes that he will do anything he can—except sin—to win individuals to Christ. What do you think about that?

_____

_____

_____

_____

_____

GETTING IT RIGHT

Sometimes we get set in our ways and comfortable with our surroundings. If new people come into our circle of friends, we may be jealous and not want to include them. Or we may not want to change the way that we do certain things to include people who are different from us.

List some of the lengths that Paul was willing to go to bring others closer to God.

_____

_____

_____

_____

_____

_____

Are you flexible enough to change the way you do things so that others can learn more about God? Why or why not?

_____

_____

_____

_____

_____

_____

_____

_____

_____

_____

LIVING IT OUT

Take a look at the list you made in the previous section. Select one way that you can be more adaptable to help others know God. Make this one thing your priority for your day.

_____

_____

_____

_____

_____

TALKING TO GOD

As you pray, think about verse 23. The gospel is the good news of eternal life. Sharing in its blessing means that we will spend eternity with those that we help win to God. Pray that God will help you influence your friends for eternity—be prepared to try something new!

_____

_____

_____

_____

_____

OTHER THOUGHTS

_____

_____

_____

_____

A daily relationship

Have you ever thought about the different kinds of shoes that you have? Take a minute to walk into your closet. How many pairs of shoes do you have? You've probably got several pairs of shoes, all of them for a different purpose. When I look in my closet I've got dress shoes, tennis shoes, golf shoes, basketball shoes, sandals, lawn-mowing shoes and my old comfortable shoes. We wear different types of shoes for different occasions. I think that we can learn a lot from the different kinds of shoes we wear.

Dress shoes—We wear nice shoes when we dress up and want to look nice. We wear them to church, weddings, job interviews or on a first date.

Our dress shoes make us look nice, but often they are un-comfortable. While we look great, we are hurting. I think that sometimes when we talk to God, we act like everything is better than it really is. We put on a smile even though we are hurting inside. Have you ever dressed up to impress someone or to hide how you are really feeling on the inside?

Athletic shoes—We only wear athletic shoes when we are practicing or competing. We are always active when we have our soccer cleats, golf spikes or running shoes on. I have found that it's very easy to get really busy doing good things. We rush to church, to youth group, to Bible studies and small groups. In fact, we can get so active that we never really slow down and listen to God. Have you ever felt that you are too busy to really connect with God?

House shoes—We all have a pair of shoes that we wear around the house. They are the ones that you slip on when you are taking out the trash, or have to run out for just a minute. But mostly they are the ones that you lounge around in. They are comfortable and it's easy to get lazy with them on. Many people put on their house shoes when it comes to God. At first, they are excited about their faith in God. Then they settle in to church activities and their Christian friends. These people don't really grow; they just go from event to event and from Sunday to Sunday. They get lazy spiritually. Have you ever noticed that you are just spiritually coasting this way?

Everyday shoes—All of us have a favorite pair of shoes. These are the ones that we wear almost all the time. They can go anywhere and do almost everything. We rely on them every day. I am sure that this is how God wants us to relate to him. He doesn't want to have a special occasion relationship. He doesn't want us so busy that we don't have time for him. He especially doesn't want us getting spiritually lazy. God wants us to have a daily relationship with him. He wants to go everywhere and do everything with us.

I never thought that the different kinds of shoes I wore could teach me so much about my relationship with God.

ENTERING IN

Turn to Colossians 3:17 and read it. The type of shoes that should represent our relationship with God should be the ones that we wear all the time—no matter what we are doing. This verse talks about the goal of all of our actions and attitudes—to give thanks to God.

GETTING IT RIGHT

In the space provided, list the things that you do each hour of the day.

7:00 A.M. _____

8:00 A.M. _____

9:00 A.M. _____

10:00 A.M. _____

11:00 A.M. _____

12:00 P.M. _____

1:00 P.M. _____

2:00 P.M. _____

3:00 P.M. _____

4:00 P.M. _____

5:00 P.M. _____

6:00 P.M. _____

7:00 P.M. _____

8:00 P.M. _____

9:00 P.M. _____

10:00 P.M. _____

11:00 P.M. _____

As you look back over the list, what are some of the things that you do not do in Jesus' name?

_____

_____

_____

_____

_____

_____

_____

_____

_____

What are some of the things that are done in Jesus' name?

_____

_____

_____

_____

_____

_____

_____

_____

_____

_____

_____

LIVING IT OUT

Which times in your week get wasted the most? When do you find it easy to get spiritually lazy?

_____

_____

_____

_____

_____

_____

_____

Pick out one thing that you do on a regular basis that you know does not give thanks to God. Make a commitment, with God's help, to work toward not doing that anymore.

_____

_____

_____

_____

_____

_____

_____

_____

TALKING TO GOD

Have a conversation with God. Ask for his strength to obey him and for your actions to be pleasing to him.

_____

_____

_____

_____

_____

_____

_____

_____

_____

_____

OTHER THOUGHTS

_____

_____

_____

_____

_____

_____

_____

_____

_____

DAY 26 | CLOSET
The ultimate refuge

I love my bedroom closet. All of my clothes are in there, and without clothes, my life would be a very different one! When I was younger, my closet was a great place to hide some of the junk that accumulated in my room. About once a week my mom would say, "Go clean up your room!" I'd go in there and mess around, and then I'd hear her say, "I'm coming up in five minutes to inspect your room!" That would motivate me to make quick progress. And since folding and hanging up clothes took way too long, I'd open my closet doors and shove everything in there that could possibly fit.

When my mom got to my room a few minutes later for the inspection, I would stand in front of the closet doors hoping that she wouldn't look inside. But she was too wise for that and most of the time she looked. I usually ended up having to pull everything out and start cleaning all over again.

More important than being a place to stash my stuff, my closet was my refuge, my place to get away from the world and sort things out. (I even hid in there during a tornado watch once, since we didn't have a basement.) My closet had one long clothing bar in it, and it had a bookcase against the back wall. If I crawled into the closet and past the bookcase, I could sit way back in there by myself and do some thinking.

Maybe I'd had a bad day at school. Maybe I'd messed up in a major way. Maybe I'd played poorly in a game. Maybe I'd had an argument with a friend. Whatever the reason, my closet was the perfect hiding place. I could crawl in there to think things through, talk to myself or talk to God.

I clearly remember crawling into the back of my closet one Saturday afternoon after a soccer game. I had made a critical mistake during the game, which allowed the other team to score the winning goal. I knew that I had blown it, and it was obvious to my teammates and my coach as well. I felt awful, so when I got home, I headed straight for my safe place—my closet.

After a while I came crawling out, squinting at the light, but feeling much better about the situation. I realized that everyone makes mistakes and that it's just another part of sports and life—God doesn't expect perfection from us. I also realized that I needed to work harder and listen to my coach more carefully—just like I needed to spend more quality time listening to God.

Don't you wish that there were a place that you could go and sort things out? Don't you wish that you had a refuge? Wouldn't it be great if every one of us had a hiding place where we would be protected from trouble?

Whether you realize it or not, you've been given access to the ultimate place of refuge—and I'm not talking about your closet.

ENTERING IN

Do you have a hiding place or safe place that you go to when you need to be alone and think? Where is it? Turn to Psalm 32:7 and read it.

_____

_____

_____

_____

GETTING IT RIGHT

When you read that God is your hiding place and that he will protect you, what are your thoughts?

_____

_____

_____

_____

_____

_____

_____

_____

_____

_____

_____

Have you ever experienced God's protection during a dangerous situation? What was it?

_____

_____

_____

_____

_____

_____

Have you ever cried out to God to protect or rescue you? How did he answer?

_____

_____

_____

_____

_____

_____

_____

_____

_____

_____

_____

_____

_____

_____

LIVING IT OUT

Today's verse says that God is our hiding place and that he will protect us. It goes on to say that he will surround us with songs of victory. Imagine that you are writing a song or poem of protection from God's perspective. Write a couple of lines that you think God would want you to hear.

_____

_____

_____

_____

_____

_____

_____

_____

_____

You don't have to wait for a dangerous time to come along to go to your hiding place. Think about some times in your week when it would be good to look for God's protection.

_____

_____

_____

_____

_____

_____

_____

_____

TALKING TO GOD

As you spend a few minutes in prayer, thank God for being your refuge and protector. Don't forget to thank him for his song—written for you and your escape.

_____

_____

_____

_____

_____

_____

_____

_____

_____

OTHER THOUGHTS

_____

_____

_____

_____

_____

_____

_____

_____

_____

DAY 27 | BED
Moments of rest

I always looked forward to Spring Break. Not only did I get a week away from school, but my youth group took a camping trip every year. We'd usually go to a state park and spend three or four days camping, hiking, cooking and just being away from home.

I loved almost everything about those trips—making foil packet dinners and campfire pies, following maps and discovering new hiking trails, getting to know people that I didn't usually spend time with. But there was one part of the camping trips that I never really liked—sleeping on the ground. Even though I'd bring a sleeping bag and an air mattress, and we did sleep inside tents, I never got a good night's rest. I'd have trouble falling asleep, and then I'd wake up extremely early and toss and turn for hours. By the end of the trip each year I'd be more than ready to dive into my warm, soft, dry, clean-smelling, flat bed.

When you think about it, we sleep in a lot of different places. We sleep at our grandparents' houses. We sleep in tents when we go camping. We sleep in hotels when we're on vacation. We spend the night at friends' houses. We sleep in cars—when someone else is driving—and we sleep on airplanes. Some of us are even guilty of sleeping during class. We can sleep almost anywhere. But there is no place like our own beds to get some serious rest.

God created the earth and everything in it in just six days, and then on the seventh day he rested. Now I don't think that God was actually tired—he's God. He's not like us. But I think that he was setting an example for us. Rest is important for our bodies, our emotions and our relationships with friends, family and even God. Rest gives us a chance to spend some time thinking about him, instead of rushing around like crazy people.

God set aside one day for us to rest and focus on him. He called that day the Sabbath. We celebrate the Sabbath on Sunday. God made it clear that we need to rest. So the next time you are lying on your bed, staring at the ceiling and thinking how good it feels just to rest, thank God for it. It was his idea first.

ENTERING IN

Read Exodus 20:8-11. God blessed the Sabbath day as a day of rest. He showed us the importance of resting by setting the example. Do you observe a day of rest to focus on God?

_____

_____

_____

_____

Why or why not?

_____

_____

_____

_____

GETTING IT RIGHT

Make a list of ways that you rest and focus on God.

_____

_____

_____

_____

_____

_____

If you had a hard time coming up with anything, what do you think God is trying to help you learn by the verses that you just read out of Exodus?

_____

_____

_____

_____

_____

LIVING IT OUT

Resting for an entire day is almost impossible. So maybe taking 100 percent of Sunday to rest and focus on God is really hard to do. But what if you could take several mini-Sabbaths throughout the day? What would you do, or not do?

_____

_____

_____

_____

_____

_____

_____

How would you focus on God?

_____

_____

_____

_____

TALKING TO GOD

Instead of working hard to come up with a prayer, just ask God to allow you to rest in him for the next few minutes. Ask him to guide your thoughts. Don't think about anything you have to do, or have done—just allow God to direct your thoughts. Close out your time by thanking him for your moment of Sabbath rest.

_____

_____

_____

OTHER THOUGHTS

_____

_____

_____

DAY 28 | STUFFED ANIMALS
Your source of comfort

Stuffed animals are a huge cultural phenomenon. You can buy them almost anywhere—in drugstores, grocery stores, superstores and specialty shops. You can even build your own bear and accessorize it. I'd guess that nearly everyone you know has had at least one stuffed animal. Some of you may still have a favorite stuffed animal. It may have been given to you by a parent, a grandparent or a really good friend. Chances are that it has a special place in your room. It might be on your dresser, on a chair or propped up on a pillow on your bed. Some of you may even still sleep with a stuffed animal.

I'll never forget the time when I was going on a mission trip to the Navajo Indian Reservation in Dilkon, Arizona. One of the girls on the trip, Jessica, brought her favorite stuffed animal. It was a fuzzy, red, bear-like animal that she called Mr. E. She didn't want anyone to know that she had brought him with her, so she tried to keep Mr. E hidden in her sleeping bag. But a couple of days into the trip, one of the other girls staying in her room saw Jessica sleeping with Mr. E. That night during dinner it "accidentally" came up that Jessica had a stuffed animal with her on the trip.

This fact did not go unnoticed by a couple of the boys on the trip. They bribed some of Jessica's roommates so that they could "borrow" Mr. E for a little while. When Jessica realized that Mr. E was missing, she was distraught.

The guys started leaving ransom notes demanding chocolate chip cookies and soft drinks in exchange for his safe return. The boys even made a video called, "Mr. E on the Reservation." It depicted an entire day in the life of a stuffed animal on a mission trip. Even Jessica had to admit that it was quite creative. And in the end, Mr. E was returned safely to Jessica, and she was able to sleep at night comforted by the knowledge that he was right by her side.

Wouldn't it be great if we could feel that same comfort when we get older—without sleeping with small, fuzzy, stuffed creatures? How awesome it would be to always feel safe and never feel alone! Well, we can. Those are things that God wants us to experience in him—not in stuffed animals.

ENTERING IN

In much the same way that a stuffed animal provides comfort and courage for a child, God promises to reassure us. See what Psalm 23 has to say about this.

_____

_____

_____

_____

_____

_____

_____

_____

_____

GETTING IT RIGHT

Go back and reread Psalm 23, only this time write down the phrases that describe God's companionship, comfort and protection.

_____

_____

_____

_____

_____

_____

_____

_____

_____

_____

_____

_____

_____

_____

Look back over your list. How does it make you feel to know that God will do all of those things?

_____

_____

_____

_____

LIVING IT OUT

In light of the fact that God is our shepherd, and that he walks with us and protects us, how can you respond to him this day?

How will knowing that God is always there change your day?

_____

_____

_____

_____

_____

_____

_____

_____

_____

What situation will you face in which you will need to rely on God's
comfort, guidance or protection?

_____

_____

_____

_____

_____

_____

_____

_____

_____

_____

_____

TALKING TO GOD

Start off by thanking God for always being with you, guiding your life, protecting you, blessing you and loving you. Express to him how important your relationship with him is to you. Choose a specific instance when you have felt his presence and thank him for it.

_____

_____

_____

_____

_____

_____

_____

_____

_____

_____

_____

OTHER THOUGHTS

_____

_____

_____

_____

_____

_____

_____

DAY 29 | AWARDS
Eternal treasure

My bedroom used to double as my trophy room. I hung my track jersey and medals on the wall. I kept my soccer varsity letter displayed proudly on a shelf. My third-place ribbon from the science fair hung from the post on my bed. But the award that was most significant to me was a plaque.

I didn't win this award for playing a sport. I received this plaque from my years in the school band. The inscription read, "Band Service Award, given to Michael Kast for excellence in serving others." Each year the award was voted on by the members of the band and given to someone who had made a difference to the band. I was so proud of it that I hung it on the wall in my room. I really valued that award and wanted other people to see it.

But over time the award lost its significance. Eventually the dusty, gold-finished plaque got stuffed in a box and stashed in my bedroom closet. It stayed there until one day I was forced to clean out my room under threat of all of my belongings ending up in a dumpster.

As I brushed off the dust, I thought about how ironic it was that an award I had prized so much ended up in a box in my bedroom closet. It had gone from being displayed on the wall to being crammed in the bottom of a box without a moment's hesitation on my part.

I started to think that there are many things in life like that trophy—things that were really important to us, but only for a short while. These things usually don't have any real value, but God has a prize for us that doesn't fade.

ENTERING IN

Read Philippians 3:12-14. Trophies are awards that are given to us for excelling. We might do well in athletics, academics or areas of service. Most of these awards mean a lot when they are given, but their importance often fades. What trophies would you like to win?

What is the prize that God offers us?

How much do you want this prize?

GETTING IT RIGHT

What do you think God is trying to tell you about the trophies that you have been given or are striving for right now?

_____

_____

_____

_____

_____

_____

_____

_____

_____

LIVING IT OUT

How can you stay focused on the trophy that will last forever?

_____

_____

_____

_____

_____

_____

_____

_____

TALKING TO GOD

Take a few minutes to talk to God. Ask him to help you compete for lasting trophies, not temporary prizes.

OTHER THOUGHTS

30 | TV

Keeping your life pure

I t used to seem like everything I did was controlled by my parents' rules. That's one of the reasons I spent so much time with my best friend, Steve. Steve's mom and dad were divorced, and he and his brother lived with his mom just down the street from me. Steve's mom wasn't around very much, and she let him do whatever he wanted. So I got to do anything I wanted when I hung out with Steve.

Steve's mom bought him a car when he got his license, and he gave me a ride home from school almost everyday. I loved going over to Steve's house after school. Steve and his family had cable and they had all the great movie channels. Steve even had a TV in his room so we spent hours watching movies and eating snacks without anyone bothering us. I thought that Steve had the best life in the world.

One weekend in October I spent the night at Steve's house. It was our plan to watch movies all weekend. Because Halloween was a few days away, one of the movie channels was showing a marathon of the scariest movies. I knew that my parents wouldn't allow me to watch these movies at home, so we decided to stay up all night watching them at his house.

I don't remember how many movies we saw that night, but I do know that we hung in there all night long and watched the whole marathon. I remember going home the next day and, besides being really tired, I was a little sad and disappointed in myself. The whole day I felt guilty that I had spent so much time watching movies that were filled with curse words, violence and murder. I knew that my actions didn't please God.

For the next several days, I remembered violent scenes. I felt bad that I had excitedly watched all those movies. After praying about it, I decided that I had to talk to Steve about how I felt. So I gathered my courage and we had a talk one day riding home from school. I explained to him that I loved hanging out with him and watching TV, but that I had to stop watching the kinds of movies that we had seen the other night. I was afraid that Steve would be upset with me, but the opposite was true. He agreed that we had made some bad choices and said that he had had a hard time getting the images out of his mind as well. It all worked out well—now we just stay up all night watching ESPN!

If you have a TV in your room, you may be tempted to watch things that you wouldn't even think of watching if your parents were in the room with you. But we have to be careful about the things we watch and the images that we put into our minds. We can honor God by keeping our lives pure.

ENTERING IN

Now read Psalm 119:37. What does this verse tell us to do? What should we fill our lives with instead of worthless things?

_____

_____

_____

_____

_____

_____

GETTING IT RIGHT

How do you think that God is trying to connect with you today about keeping your life pure? Write down a couple of thoughts that you have.

_____

_____

_____

_____

_____

_____

_____

_____

_____

_____

LIVING IT OUT

If something worthless or violent comes on when you are watching TV, change the channel or turn off the TV. If you and your friends start gossiping about someone, have the courage to confront the situation. Keep a mental list throughout your day of the number of times you have to change what you are doing in order to keep your life pure. Write here some things that end up on your list.

_____

_____

_____

_____

_____

At the end of the day, were you amazed by the amount of worthless things that you were exposed to? Why or why not?

_____

_____

_____

_____

_____

_____

_____

TALKING TO GOD

Pray that God will give you the courage to turn away from things that are worthless. Ask him to help you see with new eyes what is worthless and what is good.

_____

_____

_____

_____

_____

OTHER THOUGHTS

_____

_____

_____

SCRIPTURE REFERENCES | IN BIBLICAL ORDER

[Guys.]

What's floating around in their heads?
What makes them tick?
What makes them like you?

Secrets about Guys
[that shouldn't be secret]

**Real stories. Practical tips. Biblical advice.
Reveals secrets about guys that girls want to know!**

This book helps girls understand why guys think the way they do,
how that affects girls, and how girls can relate to guys in a way that
pleases God.

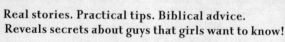